YOUR KNOWLEDGE HAS VALUE

Bibliographic information published by the German National Library:

The German National Library lists this publication in the National Bibliography; detailed bibliographic data are available on the Internet at http://dnb.dnb.de .

Imprint:

Copyright © 2017 GRIN Verlag
Print and binding: Books on Demand GmbH, Norderstedt Germany
ISBN: 9783668613089

This book at GRIN:

https://www.grin.com/document/386836

Prayag Tiwari

Accident Analysis by Using Data Mining Techniques

GRIN Verlag

GRIN - Your knowledge has value

Since its foundation in 1998, GRIN has specialized in publishing academic texts by students, college teachers and other academics as e-book and printed book. The website www.grin.com is an ideal platform for presenting term papers, final papers, scientific essays, dissertations and specialist books.

Visit us on the internet:

http://www.grin.com/

http://www.facebook.com/grincom

http://www.twitter.com/grin_com

Ministry of Education and Science of
the Russian Federation

Accident Analysis by using Data Mining Techniques

A thesis Submitted
In Fulfillment of the Requirement for the Msc

Prayag Tiwari

The Department of Computer Science and Engineering
(College of IT & Automated Control Systems)
National University Of Science And Technology "MISIS", Moscow
June 2017

Abstract

Accident data analysis is one of the prime interests in the present era. Analysis of accident is very essential because it can expose the relationship between the different types of attributes that commit to an accident. Road, traffic and airplane accident data have different nature in comparison to other real world data as accidents are uncertain. Analyzing diverse accident dataset can provide the information about the contribution of these attributes which can be utilized to deteriorate the accident rate. Nowadays, Data mining is a popular technique for examining the accident dataset. In this study, Association rule mining, different classification, and clustering techniques have been implemented on the dataset of the road, traffic accidents, and an airplane crash. Achieved result illustrated accuracy at a better level and found many different hidden circumstances that would be helpful to deteriorate accident ratio in near future.

Keywords: road and traffic accident, airplane crash, data mining, clustering techniques, classification techniques, association rule mining, accident rate

Acknowledgement

While writing my MSc dissertation I have been immensely fortunate to be surrounded by inspiring people, whose special contribution to this dissertation I would like to acknowledge.

Firstly, I am very thankful to my supervisor, Prof. D.V. Kalitin for his assistance at NUST "MISIS". I really appreciate his support that he allowed me to do independent work for my MSc dissertation.

I would like to give special thanks to the people closest to my heart: my family. My deepest love and gratitude to my parents for being the most wonderful parents in the world, I can never thank them enough for the motivation, support and for the many sacrifices they made so that I can achieve the best in my life.

I would like to thanks especially my friends Dr. Sachin Kumar and Dr. Vijay Bhaskar Semwal for always inspiring, supporting me and they are my mentor. Last but not the least I bow to the God Almighty for making these studies a successful one.

Prayag Tiwari

NUST "MISIS", Moscow

Table of Contents

List of Figures:

List of Tables:

Chapter 1

INTRODUCTION

1.1 Background

The accident has been the major reason for untimely death as well as damage to property and economic losses around the world. There are a lot of people die every year in a different type of accident. Hence, traffic authority gives generous attempt to reduce the accident but still, there is no such lessening in accident rate since in these analyzed years. The accident is unpredictable and undetermined. Hence, analysis of accident requires the comprehension of circumstance which is affecting them. Data Mining [1, 2, 28, 29, 30] has pulled in a lot of consideration in the IT industries as well as in public arena because of the extensive accessibility of vast quantity of data. So, it's necessary to transform these data into applicable knowledge and information. This applicable knowledge and information may be utilized to implement in different areas such as marketing, road accident analysis fraud detection and so on [8].

Road and traffic accident are one of the critical issues over the world. Lessening accident proportion is the best to approach to enhance traffic safety. There are diverse research has been done in many countries in traffic and road accident analysis by utilizing a different type of data mining approaches. Many researchers proposed their work in order to deteriorate the accident ratio by identifying risk factors which particularly impact in the accident [3-7].

Transportation frameworks itself is not in charge of these diverse crashes but rather a few different circumstances [12, 13]. These circumstances can be characterized as natural elements, for example, climate and temperature, road particular circumstances, for example, street sort, street width, and street bear width, human circumstances i.e. wrong side driving, abundance driving velocity and different variables. At whatever point an accident occurred in any street over the world, some of these accident circumstances are included. Likewise, these factors and their impact on the accident are not comparative in all nations; but rather they affected each accident in various nations in various ways.

Several works [14-18] have concentrated on recognizable proof of these factors so that connection between accident variables and accident severity can be built up. This connection can be used to conquer the accident rate by giving some preventive measures. Accident analysis is generally known as street and activity security in which result of accident investigation can be used for car crash avoidance

Data mining [9] is a mutative method which has been utilizing in the area of transportation. Although Barai [10] expressed that there is the different approach of information retrieval in the engineering field of transportation, for example, pavement examination, road surface investigation etc. Data mining involves numerous techniques, for example, preprocessing, association rule mining, classification, clustering and so forth.

Airplane crashes are dubious and erratic occurrences and their examination requires the information of the variables influencing them. Airplane crashes are characterized by an arrangement of factors which are for the most part of discrete nature. The real issue in the investigation of accident information is its heterogeneous nature. In this manner heterogeneity must be considered amid an analysis of the information generated, some association between the information may stay covered up. Despite the fact that, analysts utilized division of the information to diminish this heterogeneity utilizing a few measures, for example, expert learning, however, there is no certification that this will prompt an ideal division which comprises of homogeneous gatherings of an airplane crash. In this way, cluster analysis may help the division of airplane crashes.

The aircraft organizations are one of the fields, with the fast development in air travel, cancellations, flight deferrals, and occurrences have likewise significantly expanded in late years. Therefore, there is a lot of information and information aggregation in the aeronautics business. This information could be put away as pilot reports, sup-port reports, occurrence reports, segment reports or postpone reports. Likewise in the flight business, information mining applications have been performed.

1.2 Overview of Data Mining Techniques

Data Mining is characterized as the strategy of retrieving data from big sets of data. As such, we can state that data mining is mining information from data.

1.2.1 Clustering

Clustering is the gathering of a specific arrangement of objects on the basis of their features, grouping them as indicated by their resemblance. What makes a contrast between clustering and classification is that in classification, every record allocated a pre-defined class in according to an enhanced model alongside training on the pre-classified cases and also clustering does not rely on upon predefined classes [11].

a. Application of Clustering Analysis

- Clustering approach is comprehensively utilized as a part of numerous applications, for example, pattern recognition, image processing, market research, data analysis.
- Clustering can likewise enable advertisers to find unmistakable gatherings in their client base. What's more, they can portray their client group on the pattern for purchasing.

- In the area of biology, it can be utilized to determine plant and creature taxonomies, categorize genes with comparative functionalities and pick up knowledge into structures inalienable to populations.
- Clustering likewise helps in the finding of areas of comparative land use in an earth perception database. It additionally helps in the recognition of gatherings of houses in a city as indicated by house sort, value, and geographic area.
- Clustering likewise helps in grouping documents on the web for data retrieval.
- Clustering is additionally utilized as a part of anomaly identification applications, for example, fraud detection in credit card.

b. Prerequisites of Clustering in Data Mining

- Scalability
- High dimensionality
- Ability to manage various type of attributes
- Interpretability
- Ability to manage with noisy kind of data

1.2.2 Classification

Classification is a data mining approach that allocates things in a gathering to class or target categories. The objective of classification is to precisely predict the targeted class for each case in the dataset. For instance, a classification model could be utilized to distinguish loan candidates as high, medium and low credit risks.

a. Classifications Issues

Preparing the data is major issue for classification and prediction. There are following steps involved in preparing the data

- Data Cleansing

- Data transformation and reduction
- Relevance Analysis

1.2.3 Association rule mining

Association rule mining is essentially centered on finding continuous co-happening associations among a gathering of things. It is at times alluded to as "Market Basket Analysis" since that was the first application territory of association mining. The objective is to discover associations between things that happen together more frequently than you would anticipate from an irregular inspecting of all conceivable outcomes. The great case of this is the well-known Beer and Diapers association that is frequently said in data mining books. The story goes this way: men who go to the store to purchase diapers will likewise tend to purchase beer in the meantime [23].

1.3 Challenges in accident

The fundamental concern with accident data investigation is to recognize the most persuasive feature influencing accident recurrence and seriousness of the accident. The real issue with accident dataset analysis is its heterogeneous behavior. Heterogeneity in accident data is exceedingly undesirable and unavoidable [19]. The real inconvenience of heterogeneity of accident data is that sure connections may stay concealed, for example, certain accident features related with specific vehicle sort may not be significant in the whole informational index; the immensity of the impact of certain accident-related variables might be diverse for different conditions; seriousness levels for an accident contributing circumstances might be distinctive for various accident sorts. This heterogeneous behavior of accident data may prompt less precise outcome [20]. So as to get more precise outcomes, this heterogeneity of street accident data must be expelled. Keeping in mind the end goal to manage this heterogeneous nature of accident data, a few reviews [21, 22], partition the information into gatherings in light of some exogenous traits e.g. accident area, street condition, reason for accident and so on and broke down each gathering independently to recognize a few powerful variables related with accident in each gathering. Be that as it may, this decision is doubtful as gathering, the information in light of specific characteristics may bring about less critical gatherings.

1.4 Objective

The overall objective of this thesis is to achieve the accuracy and identify the factors behind crashes or accident that could be helpful to reduce accident ratio in near future and could be helpful to save many lives, deteriorate wealth destruction as well as many other things. In next section, Overview of research articles related from this thesis has been mentioned.

1.5 Organization of Thesis

The result of this thesis is based on 5 research articles and structure of thesis would be as follow with a short description of each research article in this section.

In a 1st research article, different clustering, classification techniques as well association rule mining used to find the correlation between diverse factors. In the first research articles, K-modes clustering, Self-Organizing Map (SOM) technique has been utilized to group the data into homogeneous segments and then applied Naive Bayes (NB), Decision tree, Support vector machine (SVM) to classify the dataset. It has been performed classification on data with and without clustering. The result illustrates that superior classification accuracy can be achieved after segmentation of data using clustering [24].

14

In a 2nd research article, it has been proposed a different classification and clustering techniques to analyze data. There are various implemented classification techniques such as Lazy classifier, Decision Tree, and Multilayer Perceptron classifier to classify a bunch of dataset on the basis of casualty class as well as clustering techniques which are Hierarchical and k-means clustering techniques to cluster whole dataset. Firstly, Dataset was analyzed by utilizing these classifiers and accomplished precision at some level and later, Clustering approach was implemented and after that implemented classification approaches on that clustered dataset. Achieved precision level enhanced at some level by utilizing clustering on dataset contrasted with a dataset which was classified without clustering [23]

In a 3rd research article, it has been presented a conjoint analysis using k-mode clustering and Bayesian Networks on an imbalanced road accident data from Leeds, UK. The motivation of this study was to validate the performance of classification before and after the clustering process [25].

In a 4th research article, It has been performed a comparative study using k-modes, LCC and BIRCH (Balanced Iterative Reducing and Clustering using Hierarchies) clustering techniques over a new multi-vehicular accidents data from Muzzafarnagar, Uttar Pradesh, India. Further, applied Naïve Bayes (NB) algorithm to predict the severity of traffic and road accidents for each of the clusters obtained. The cause behind the selection of Naïve Bayes algorithm for classification is that several data tuples are their which contains the similar attribute values for different class values or dependent attribute value. In such cases, decision tree technique usually fails (Tan et al., 2006). Therefore, it has been selected NB technique as it classifies the data tuple based on the probability values. The results revealed that prediction accuracy for NB, SVM, and RF are found higher for the clusters attained from LCC whereas for the clusters obtained from BIRCH the prediction accuracy was comparatively low than LCC and k-modes clusters. On the other side, the computation speed of k-modes is found higher than both LCC and BIRCH. The organization of rest of the paper is as follows: Next section focused on literature survey, materials and methods used in the study that comprise of a brief overview of the data set being utilized in the study and various techniques that have been utilized in the study [26].

In a 5th research article, this paper proposes a system that depends on the cluster investigation utilizing hierarchical clustering and association rule mining utilizing Apriori technique. Utilizing cluster investigation as a preparatory undertaking can gather the information into various homogeneous portions. Association rule is additionally connected to these groups and additionally on the whole dataset to produce association rules. In the best of insight, it is the first occasion when that both the methodologies have been utilized together for investigation of a dataset of a road accident. The consequence of the investigation demonstrates that utilizing cluster analysis as a preparatory assignment can help in expelling heterogeneity to some degree in the dataset of a road accident [27]. Chapter 4-5 will discuss the experiment and results which are followed by a conclusion and recommendation section.

Chapter 2

LITERATURE SURVEY

2.1 Introduction

Accident analysis is an essential area of study in the transportation domain (Kumar and Toshniwal, 2016a). Various studies used statistical methods (Savolainen et al., 2010; Karlaftis and Tarko, 1998; Jones et al., 1991, Poch and Mannering, 1996, Maher and Summersgill, 1996) and data mining techniques (Kumar and Toshniwal, 2015a, 2016b, 2016c; Chang and Chen, 2005; Kashani et al., 2011, Prayag et al., 2017) to analyze traffic accident data and establishing relationships between accident attributes and road accident severity. The results obtained from these studies are very useful as different circumstances affecting road accidents are revealed. Awareness of these accident factors is certainly helpful in taking preventive measures to overcome the accident rates in the area of study [37-41, 32, 7, 19, 42-43, 79, 80].

2.2 Factors responsible for accident

A review by Peng and Boyle [59] tried to pick up bits of knowledge on the impact of commercial driver considers on crash seriousness regarding run-of-road (ROR), single-vehicle crashes. This review said safety belt utilize essentially lessened the probability of damage and deadly ROR crashes. Driver diversion and heedlessness improved the probability of an ROR crash. Fatigue, Laziness and speeding fundamentally improved the probability of harm and lethal ROR crashes. Commercial motor vehicle (CMV) drivers who drove a non-damaged truck were related with a lower probability of harm and deadly ROR crashes. An ROR crash was around 3.8 times more prone to be harmful and deadly on the off chance that it occurred on provincial streets or dry streets.

No other informative factors were seen as critical. The consequences of this review propose that few driver elements: fatigue and laziness, speeding, diversion, distractedness, and safety belt utilize influenced the probability of an ROR crash being injurious. Hence, the investigation of Peng and Boyle [59] gives bits of knowledge on the greatness of the impact of these driver calculates on ROR crashes that include huge trucks. The outcomes have suggestions for behavioral security countermeasures that can help relieve the effects of driver diversions and speeding.

Transient circumstances identified with the inability to recognize vehicle may incorporate liquor, fatigue/absence of rest, negligence, and data over-burden, while elements that are more lasting may incorporate "intellectual" conspicuity and field reliance [60]. The model with the better fitting and most elevated prescient ability was utilized to identify the impact of the roadway, an ecological issue, vehicle, and driver related circumstances on severity. Gadget utilization, travel speed, purpose of effect, utilization of drugs and liquor, individual situation, regardless of whether the driver is to blame, sex, curve/grade and rural/urban nature presence at the crash area were distinguished as the critical elements for having a harm severity effect to older drivers muddled in single-vehicle accidents [61]. Logistic regression was implemented to crash-related information gathered from traffic police records keeping in mind the end goal to inspect the involvement of several circumstances to the severity of accident [62]. The requested probit model was utilized to compute the impact of the roadway and zone sort factors on injury seriousness of pedestrian crash in a rural area [63]. Inability to wear safety belts did not anticipate crashes but rather did altogether impact the seriousness of crashes that occurred; that is, the individuals who had before revealed utilizing safety belts "always" were more improbable than others to be harmed when the crash occurred. Budgetary anxiety increased the probability of inclusion in a more dangerous accident [64]. These outcomes will impact the urban movement police authorization measures, which will change the improper conduct of drivers and secure the minimum experienced street users.

There are many factors responsible for an accident like driver alcohol and drug involvement, the age of the driver, improper driving education, other vehicle driver experience, urban/rural nature, speed, environmental issue, runway, engine problem, pilot fault etc.

2.3 Traditional Statistical approach for accident analysis

Statistical techniques or "statistics" are not data mining approaches. They were being utilized sometime before the term data mining was begotten to apply to business applications. Notwithstanding, statistical approaches are driven by the information and are utilized to find a pattern and make predictive models.

Statistical approaches have also played an important role in road safety research. Karlaftis and Tarko (1998) studied the impact of age of riders on accident patterns. They used negative binomial models along with cluster analysis to analyze the road accident data. Several important studies (Savolainen et al., 2010; Karlaftis and Tarko, 1998; Jones et al., 1991, Poch and Mannering, 1996) using statistical techniques have been performed on road accident data.

Lord and Mannering (2010) provided a detailed survey of the key issues related to crash-recurrence information and the weakness and strengths of the diverse methodological techniques that scientists have utilized to address these issues. While the consistent march of methodological advancement (consisting recent utilizations of the finite mixture model and random parameter) has considerably enhanced our comprehension of circumstances that influence crash-frequencies, it is the anticipation of joining developing approaches with much more point by point vehicle crash information that holds the better promise of what's to come in near future [65].

Poch and Mannering (1996) Utilized seven-year accident dataset from 63 intersections in Bellevue, Washington (all of which were focused on operational changes), this paper evaluates a negative binomial regression of the recurrence of crashes at crossing point approaches. The estimation comes about reveal imperative intersections amongst traffic and geometric related factors and crash frequencies. The motivation of this paper gives exploratory methodological and exact proof that could prompt a way to deal with gauge the accident lessening advantages of different proposed upgrades on operationally lacking intersections [66].

However, it is found in several studies (Ona et al., 2013; Kumar and Toshniwal, 2016d) that clustering improves the performance of classification or prediction. Latent class clustering has been widely utilized for cluster analysis in traffic and road accident dataset whereas k-modes clustering has also been used in few studies. Although every clustering technique has its own advantage and limitations, it usually depends on the choice of authors to select any clustering algorithm that suits best for the data. Therefore, it is required to estimate the execution of clustering techniques on explicit frameworks such as clustering efficiency based on computation speed and clustering result [7, 32 19, 42-43].

2.4 Data Mining approaches for Accident Analysis

Kumar and Toshniwal (2015a) proposed a framework to remove the heterogeneity from the road accident data and suggested that clustering prior to analysis is very useful to manage with the heterogeneity of traffic and road accident data. Ona et al. (2013) used latent class clustering (LCC) technique to remove heterogeneity from the data. They suggested that LCC is very useful clustering technique and also provides different cluster selection criteria to be used for identifying a number of clusters present in the data set. Further, (Kumar and Toshniwal, 2016d) performed a comparative study on road accident data from Haridwar, Uttarakhand, India. In this study, they used LCC and K-modes (Chaturvedi et al., 2001; Kumar and Toshniwal, 2015b) clustering techniques to cluster the data prior to performing the analysis. Further, they extracted association rules using Frequent Pattern (FP) growth technique to extract the rules that described accident pattern in each cluster. They concluded that both techniques have similar efficiency on cluster formation and are able to remove the heterogeneity from the data. However, their findings were not suitable to reveal the superiority of one technique over other.

Karlaftis and Tarko [19] used the investigation to cluster the data and afterward sorted that dataset of the accident into individual categories and additionally clustered output of investigated dataset by utilizing Negative Binomial (NB) to identify the reason of accident by centering age of driver which may exhibit a few outcomes.

Kwon OH [45] used Naive Bayes and Decision Tree classification approach to analyzing aspect dependencies related with safety of the road. Youthful Sohn [46] utilized an alternate algorithm to improve the accuracy of various classifiers for two severity categories of a traffic accident and every classifier utilized the neural network and decision tree. Tibebe [47] built up a classification model for Traffic officers at Addis Ababa Traffic office that could help them for taking the decision to manage traffic connected activities in Ethiopia. S. Kuznetsov et al. [48-50] used an algorithm based on FCA for numerical data mining and provided more efficient results.

Christopher [51, 52] utilized five classification techniques on airplane crash dataset to identify the performance of every each classification techniques on a different component of aviation dataset. The primary commitment of this review is to assess the execution of various classification systems are NB, SVM, DT, NN and KNN on a component of aeronautics. In this paper, examined the significance of highlight determination strategies for enhancing the execution of order techniques. It is found that the distinctive component determination trait lessons a number of excesses and unessential qualities in this manner expand the execution of classifiers. We discover that foremost part examination based on highlight selector properties and choice tree based with a classifier is best appropriate for prediction of aircraft crashes dataset.

Bineid and Fielding utilized information mining strategies to clarify the improvement of a dispatch dependability expectation strategy for a traveler flying machine. Nazeri and Zhang depicted the utilization of information mining to investigating extreme climate impacts on the national airspace framework (CAA) was connected to achieve the review. Their approach takes the more perplexing connections among applicable execution [53-54].

P. Tiwari et al. [32] utilized machine learning techniques such as Naïve Bayes (NB), Support Vector Machine (SVM) and Maximum Entropy (ME) on Rotten Tomatoes movie dataset by utilizing n-gram approach. It is seen that precision of a classification lessened by expanding the estimation of "n" in n-gram i.e., it is noticed that outcome is optimal in the case of unigram, bigram and trigram yet exactness diminish when identified for four-gram and further on.

P. Tiwari et al. [23] used k-modes and hierarchical clustering to cluster accident data then applied classification approaches on clustered data where accuracy enhanced at some degree. S. Kumar et al. [20] utilized k-mode clustering and association rule to spot the diverse factors that are connected to the frequency of a road accident and clusters found by a k-mode clustering technique. Mama and Kockelman [44] utilized clustering as their initial step to gather the information into various portions and further, they utilized Probit model to distinguish the association between various mischance qualities. Negative binomial (NB) models [55, 56] and Poisson models [57, 58] have been utilized broadly to recognize the connection between car crashes and the causative elements. It has been broadly perceived that Poisson models outflank the standard relapse models in taking care of the non-negative, irregular and discrete components of crash counts. P. Tiwari et al. [24-26] used diverse classification approaches to examine the accuracy of different classifiers by utilizing different clustering techniques and attained accuracy at some levels on the diverse dataset [29, 30, 33, 34].

Chapter 3

METHODOLOGY AND DATA COLLECTION

3.1 Introduction

The current study analyzed road and traffic accident on a dataset of Leed City (UK) and Muzzafarnagar district (Uttar Pradesh), airplane crash dataset of Federal Aviation Administration (USA). Several machine learning approaches have been implemented to analyze dataset which is discussed in section 3.2. In Chapter 4, Results are divided into five section. Result no. 1, 2, 3 is based on a dataset of Leed City (UK), Result no. 4 is based on a dataset of Muzzafarnagar district (Uttar Pradesh) and Result no. 5 is based on a dataset of Federal Aviation Administration (USA).

3.2 Proposed Methodology

In this section, several machine learning approaches has been discussed like K-modes Clustering, Hierarchical clustering, Latent Class Clustering (LCC), Balanced Iterative Reducing and Clustering using Hierarchies (BIRCH), Support Vector Machine (SVM), Self-Organizing Map (SOM) Naïve Bayes (NB), Decision Tree, Bayesian Networks, Lazy Classifier (K-star and IBK), Multilayer Perceptron (MP) etc.

3.2.1 K-modes clustering

Clustering is an unsupervised data mining approach whose major objective is to categorize the data objects into a distinct type of clusters in such a way that objects inside a group are more alike than the objects in different clusters. K-means [67] algorithm is a very famous clustering technique for large numerical data analysis. In this, the dataset is grouped into k clusters. There are diverse clustering algorithms available but the assortment of appropriate clustering algorithm relies on type and nature of data. Our major objective of this work is to differentiate the accident location on their frequency occurrence. Let's assume that X and Y is a matrix of m by n matrix of categorical data. The straightforward closeness coordinating measure amongst X and Y is the quantity of coordinating quality estimations of the two values. The more noteworthy the quantity of matches is more the comparability of two items. K-modes [20, 36, 39] algorithm can be explained as:

$$d \qquad (X_i, Y_i) \qquad = \qquad \sum_{i=1}^{m} \delta(Xi, Yi)$$
....(1)

$$\text{Where } \delta(Xi, Yi) = \begin{cases} 1, & if\ Xi = Yi \\ 0, & if\ Xi \neq Yi \end{cases} \quad ....$$
(2)

3.2.2 Self-Organizing Map (SOM)

Self-Organizing Map (SOM) by Teuvo Kohonen [69] gives a visualization of data which assist high dimensional data by decreasing the dimension of data. SOM likewise describe clustering idea by gathering comparative data together. Thusly one might say that SOM decreases the dimension of data and presentations similitudes among dataset.

With SOM, clustering is executed by having a few units go after the present object. Once the information has been gone into the framework, the network of neurons is prepared by giving data about sources of info. The weight vector of the unit is nearest to the present object turns into the triumphant or dynamic unit. Amid the preparation organize, the values for the input factors are progressively balanced trying to safeguard neighborhood connections that exist inside the input dataset. As it gets nearer to the input object, the weights of the triumphant unit are balanced and in addition its neighbors. At the point when a training set has been forced to the neural systems than their Euclidean separation to conclusive weight, vectors are figured. Presently the neuron weight is around like the weight of input data. In this way, this is called by the triumphant unit or Best Matching Neuron (BMN). The weight of alteration decreases with separation and time from the BMN. The evaluated formula for neuron n with having weight vector Wn(s) is given as

$$Wn(s+1)= \quad Wn(s)+\theta(i, \quad n, \quad s) \quad \cdot \quad \alpha(s) \cdot \quad (F(t)- \quad Wn))$$
$$\dots\dots\dots\dots\dots\dots\dots\dots\dots.(3)$$

In this shown equation, s is stepped index, t is a record in training case, i is an index of BMN for F(t), $\alpha(s)$ is diminishing coefficient and input vector is F(t). θ (i, n, s) is the locale function which gives the space between neuron i and n in s step. As upon the implementation, t may investigate dataset reliably (t=0, 1, 2, 3, 4 - T-1 and T is the span of training).

3.2.3 Hierarchical Clustering

Hierarchical clustering is the place you construct a clustered tree to depict data (Dendrogram in Figure no. 2), where each segment (or "node") is connected to at least two successor segments. The segments are settled and sorted out as a tree, which in a perfect world winds up as a significant classification plot.

Every node in the clustered tree contains a segment of comparable data; Nodes are put on the diagram beside other, comparative nodes. The cluster at first level are joined with a cluster in the following level up, utilizing a level of likeness; the procedure carries on until all nodes are in the tree, which gives a visual preview of the information contained in the entire set. The aggregate number of cluster is not fore-ordained before you start the tree creation.

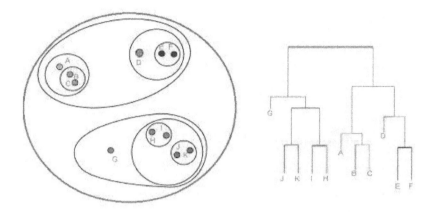

Figure 1 A dendrogram (right) depicting nested hierarchical clusters (left)

Methodologies for hierarchical clustering, for the most part, fall into two sorts:

a. Agglomerative Clustering

This is a "base up" viewpoint: every perception begins in its own particular cluster, and matches of clusters are converged as one shift the hierarchy.

- The utmost distance between component of each of the cluster is known as complete linkage clustering

$$Max \{D(X, Y): X \in A, Y \in B\} \dots\dots\dots\dots\dots\dots\dots\dots\dots\dots\dots\dots$$
(4)

- The shortest distance between component of each of the cluster is known as single linkage clustering

$$Min \{D(X, Y): X \in A, Y \in B\} \dots\dots\dots\dots\dots\dots\dots\dots\dots (5)$$

- The mean distance between component of each of the cluster is known as single linkage clustering

$$\frac{1}{|A|.|B|} \Sigma_{X \in A}. \Sigma_{Y \in B} D(X, Y) \dots\dots\dots\dots\dots\dots\dots\dots\dots (6)$$

b. Divisive Clustering

This is a "top-down" viewpoint: all perceptions start in one cluster, and parts are executed recursively as one moves down the chain of command.

3.2.4 Latent Class Clustering (LCC)

LCC is a popular clustering approach and has been widely used for analyzing road and traffic accident data. The most prominent advantage of LCC is that it can be used with any type of data such as categorical, numerical or mix attributes data. Another advantage is that LCC provides diverse cluster selection criteria like Akaike Information Criteria (AIC) (Akaike, 1987), Bayesian Information Criteria (BIC) (Raftery, 1986) and CAIC (Consistent AIC) (Fraley and Raftery, 1998) in order to identify an appropriate number of clusters to be formed. These information criterions can be expressed as in Eq. 7, 8, 9.

$$AIC = -2logL + 2n \dots\dots\dots\dots\dots\dots\dots\dots\dots\dots\dots\dots\dots\dots\dots\dots \quad (7)$$

$$BIC = -2logL + n(log(N)) \dots\dots\dots\dots\dots\dots\dots\dots\dots\dots\dots\dots \quad (8)$$

$$CAIC = -2logL + n(log(N) + 1) \dots\dots\dots\dots\dots\dots\dots\dots\dots \quad (9)$$

Where L is the maximum value of likelihood function, n is the number of model parameters and N is the sample data size. The different values of AIC, BIC and CAIC are evaluated across different cluster models to lead the number of clusters to be formed.

3.2.5 BIRCH (Balanced Iterative Reducing and Clustering using Hierarchies)

BIRCH is a popular dynamic clustering technique that used hierarchical cluster analysis over a large set of data in order to provide efficient clusters. BIRCH has an advantage over previous clustering algorithms in which large data cannot be fitted into the memory. In other words, we can say that BIRCH is a cost-effective algorithm in terms of CPU time and memory. The BIRCH algorithm is briefly discussed as follows:

- Initially, all data is scanned and an initial Clustering Feature (CF) tree is built using the memory provided and recycling space available on disk
- Compress into required length by creating smaller CF tree
- Perform hierarchical clustering
- Refine clusters obtained in order to get the optimal clusters. This is an optional step and requires more scan of the data in several passes

The more details about BIRCH algorithm can be found in a study by Zhang et al. (1996).

3.2.6 Support Vector Machine (SVM)

SVM is supervised learning method with an analogous algorithm which analyzes data for regression and classification analysis. SVM works on the basis of decision planes which explain decision boundary. Decision planes are something which differentiates across a set of objects with having distinct classes. It's a classifier technique that executes classification task by making hyperplanes in n- dimensional space which differentiates the level of classes. SVM assist classification task as well as regression task also and can manage multiple categorical as well as continuous variables.

For the classification type of SVM, minimize the error function: $(V^T V/2)$ + $C\sum_{i=1}^{N}\beta i$

Subjects to the limitations: $Y_i (V^T \theta (X_i)+b)>=1-\beta_i, \beta_i>=0, i=1,2,3,------N$ *...(10)*

Here v is vector coefficient, c which is known as capacity constant, β explain the boundary for managing non separable data which is input data and here b is constant. Here i is the index for level T cases of training set, X_i and Y_i describe the class labels and independent variables. α is generally using for transmuting data from the input data to the space feature. If C is greater than more error proscribed so C must be chosen properly.

It's the second type to reduce error function for classification type: $(V^T V/2)$ –

$v\alpha + \frac{1}{N}\sum_{i=1}^{N}\beta i$

Subjects to the limitations: $Y_i(V^T\theta(X_i)+b) >= \alpha-\beta_i,\ \beta_i >= 0,\ i=1,2,3,------N$ and $\alpha >= 0$ always .... (11)

You need to evaluate the dependent function of the y dependent factor on an arrangement of independent factors x. It accepts as other regression issues that the connection across the independent and dependent factors is provided by a deterministic function which is f in addition to the expansion of some extra noise.

Y=f(x) + some noises

For the regression type of SVM: $(V^T V/2) + C\sum_{i=1}^{N}\beta i + C\sum_{i=1}^{N}\beta'i$ .... (12)

These reduce subjects to $V^T\theta(X_i)+b-Y_i = <\varepsilon+\beta'_i$

$Y_i - V^T\theta(X_i)-b = <\varepsilon+\beta_i$

$\beta_i,\ \beta'_i >= 0,\ i=1,\ 2,\ 3 --------N$

It's the second type to reduce error function for classification type: $(V^T V/2)$

$- C\ (v\varepsilon + \frac{1}{N}\sum_{i=1}^{N}(\beta i + \beta'i))$...

(13)

$(V^T\theta(X_i)+b)-Y_i = <\varepsilon+\beta_i$

$Y_i-(V^T\theta(X_i)+b) = <\varepsilon+\beta'_i$

$\beta_i,\ \beta'_i >= 0,\ i=1,2,3 --------N,\ \varepsilon >= 0$

3.2.7 Naïve Bayes (NB)

This classifier is on the basis of Bayes' hypothesis with autonomy suspicions across indicators. This model is easier to design, with no astonishing iterative measure approximation which makes it primarily precious for large datasets. Despite its smoothness, this classifier often works very well and which is generally utilized on the grounds that it regularly outflanks more complex order techniques. Given a class variable x and element vector y1 through yn, Bayes' hypothesis expresses the accompanying relationship:

$$P(x|y_1, \ldots . y_n) = \frac{P(x)\, P(y_1, \ldots\ldots\ldots y_n\ |x)}{P(y_1 \ldots\ldots\ldots y_n)} \quad \ldots\ldots\ldots\ldots\ldots\ldots\ldots\ldots\ldots\ldots\ldots$$

(14)

By using the Naive Bayes assumption that

$$P(y_i|\ x, y_1 \ldots\ldots, y_{i-1}, \ldots\ldots, y_n) = P(y_i|x) \quad \ldots\ldots\ldots\ldots\ldots\ldots\ldots\ldots\ldots \text{ (15)}$$

for all i, this relationship is streamlined to

$$P(x|y_1, \ldots . y_n) = \frac{P(x)\prod_{i=1}^{n} P(y_i|x)}{P(y_1 \ldots\ldots\ldots y_n)} \quad \ldots\ldots\ldots\ldots\ldots\ldots\ldots\ldots\ldots\ldots\ldots$$

(16)

Since $P(y_1, \text{------}, y_n)$ is steady given the information, we can utilize the accompanying classification run the show:

$$P(x|y_1, \ldots . y_n) \propto P(x) \prod_{i=1}^{n} P(y_i|x)$$

$$\hat{x} = arg\ max\ = P(x) \prod_{i=1}^{n} P(y_i|x) \quad \ldots\ldots\ldots\ldots\ldots\ldots\ldots\ldots \text{ (18)}$$

What's more, we can utilize Maximum A Posteriori (MAP) estimation to gauge P(x) and $P(y_i|\ x)$; the previous is then the relative recurrence of class x in the preparation set. Regardless of their clearly over-improved suppositions, credulous Bayes classifiers have worked well in some circumstances, broadly dataset classification and spam separating. They require a little measure of preparing information to gauge the fundamental parameters.

3.2.8 Decision Tree

J48 is an augmentation of ID3. The additional elements of J48 are representing missing data. In the WEKA, J48 is a Java platform open source of the C4.5 calculation. The WEKA gives various alternatives connected with tree pruning. If there should arise an occurrence of possible overfitting pruning may be utilized as a tool for accuracy. Random forest are a package learning techniques for regression, classification, and other tasks, that perform by building a legion of decision trees at training time and resulting in the class which would be the mode of the mean prediction (regression) or classes (classification) of the separate trees. Random decision forests good for decision trees' routine of overfitting to their training set. In different calculations, the classification is executed recursively till each and every leaf is clean or pure, that is the order of the data ought to be as impeccable as would be prudent. The goal is dynamically speculation of a choice tree until it picks up the balance of adaptability and exactness. This technique utilized the 'Entropy' that is the computation of disorder data. Here Entropy $X^{\rightarrow}$ is measured by:

$$Entropy \ (\vec{X}) \ = \ -\sum_{i=1}^{n} \frac{|Xi|}{|\vec{X}|} log\left(\frac{|Xi|}{|\vec{X}|}\right) \ \dots\dots\dots\dots\dots\dots\dots\dots\dots\dots$$
(19)

$$Entropy \ (i|\vec{X}) \ = \frac{|Xi|}{|\vec{X}|} log\left(\frac{|Xi|}{|\vec{X}|}\right) \ \dots\dots\dots\dots\dots\dots\dots\dots\dots\dots$$
(20)

Hence,

$$Total \ Gain = Entropy \ (\vec{X}) \ -Entropy \ (i|\vec{X}) \ \dots\dots\dots\dots\dots\dots\dots\dots \ (21)$$

Here the goal is to increase the total gain by dividing total entropy because of diverging arguments $\vec{X}$ by value i.

3.2.9 Multilayer Perceptron

An MLP might be observed as a logistic regression classifier in which input data is firstly altered utilizing a non-linear transformation. In this, alteration deal the input dataset into space, and the place where this turn into linearly separable. This layer as an intermediate layer is known as a hidden layer. One hidden layer is enough to create MLPs.

Formally, a single hidden layer Multilayer Perceptron (MLP) is a function of f: YI→YO, where I would be the input size vector x and O is the size of output vector f(x), such that, in matrix notation

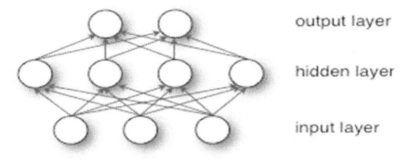

output layer

hidden layer

input layer

Figure 2 Neural Network

$$F(x) \quad = \quad g(\theta(2)+W(2)(s(\theta(1)+W(1)x))) \quad ....$$

(22)

3.2.10 Association Rule Mining

Association rule mining [30] is an exceptionally well-known data mining strategy that concentrates intriguing and shrouded relations between different qualities in a vast informational index. Association rule mining produces an arrangement of standards that characterize the basic examples in the informational collection.

The associativity of two attributes of crashes is dictated by the recurrence of their event together in the informational collection. A run $X \to Y$ demonstrates that if X happens then Y will likewise happen.

Given a dataset D of n exchanges where every exchange Tϵ D. Let I = {I1, I2,... In} is an arrangement of things. A thing set X will happen in T if and just if X $\subseteq$ T. $X \to Y$ is and affiliation manage, given that X $\subset$ I, Y $\subset$ I and X $\cap$ Y = $\emptyset$.

Agrawal and Srikant [69] proposed a calculation known as Apriori calculation to discover the affiliation rules from substantial datasets. The pseudo-code for customary affiliation administer digging calculation for incessant item set era is as per the following:

A_K = {recurrence item set of K size}

B_K = {Candidate item set of K size}

C_1 = {recurrence 1 item set}

While $(A_K-1 \neq \Phi)$ then

    B_{K+1}=candidate produced from A_K

    For every transaction t ϵ D do

        Augment the counts of candidate in B_{K+1} that also hold in t

    A_K+1= candidates in B_{K+1} with the lowest aid

    $K=K+1;$

    Return $U_K A_K$

Furthermore, an association rule is created from the successive item sets and solid principles in light of Interestingness computation are taken for the examination.

Interestingness computation

An association rule is considered as a solid control if is fulfills the base limit criteria, i.e., support and confidence. A base bolster S of a control $X \rightarrow Y$ shows that in x % of all exchanges X and Y together happens and it can be figured utilizing Eq. (23); though a certainty c of a decision shows that in c % of all exchange when A happen then B additionally happens and it can be ascertained utilizing Eq. (24). Lift is another intriguing quality measure of manage, which can be computed utilizing Eq. (25). An esteem more noteworthy than 1 for the lift measures depicts that the presence of A and B together is more than expected though an esteem lower than 1 demonstrates invert of the idea. So a control is considered as solid on the off chance that it has an esteem more noteworthy than 1 for the lift parameter.

$$Support= P \ (X \cap Y) \ \ldots\ldots\ldots\ldots\ldots\ldots\ldots\ldots\ldots\ldots\ldots\ldots\ldots\ldots$$

(23)

$$Confidence= P \ (X \mid Y) \ = \frac{P \ (X \cap Y)}{P \ (X)} \ \ldots\ldots\ldots\ldots\ldots\ldots\ldots\ldots\ldots\ldots$$

(24)

$$Lift= \frac{P \ (X \cap Y)}{(P \ (A)P \ (B))} \ \ldots\ldots\ldots\ldots\ldots\ldots\ldots\ldots\ldots\ldots\ldots\ldots\ldots\ldots\ldots$$

(25)

3.2.11 Cluster Selection Criteria

The major issue in cluster analysis is to identify the suitable number of clusters to be made out of the data. The available information criterion with LCC can be used to identify the number of clusters. We have used Gap statistic (Tibshirani et al., 2001) criteria along with AIC, BIC and CAIC information criterion for identifying an appropriate number of clusters.

Assuming a data set D_{ij}, i=1,2,...,m, j=1,2,....,n, which consists of m data objects of n attributes. Considering d_{xy} is the squared Euclidean distance between objects X and Y given by dxy = $\sum$ (Xj – Yj)2. If the data set has been grouped into k clusters, c1, c2,….,ck, where ci indicates the ith cluster, then ni = |ci|.

Let Di = $\sum$dxy, (where x, y $\in$ ci) is the sum of pairwise distances for all points in cluster i and Wk is the collective within cluster sum of squares around the cluster means and is given by Eq.(26). Gapn(k) can be defined as the difference between expected and observed values of log(Wk) and given in Eq.(27). The value maximizing Gapn(k) can be selected as a number of k.

$$W_k = \sum_{i=1}^{k} \left(\frac{1}{2n_i}\right) . D_i \dots\dots\dots (26)$$

$$Gap_n(k) = E_n^* . \{log \, W_k\} - log \, W_k \dots\dots\dots (27)$$

Where E*n denotes the expectation under a sample size n from the reference distribution.

The Gap statistic is the difference between expected Elog(Wk) and Observed log(Wk). Wk is the within-cluster sum of squared distance. The best cluster model is the one maximizing the Gap value.

3.2.12 Accuracy Measurement

The classification accuracy is one of the important measures of how correctly a classifier classifies a record to its class value? The confusion matrix is an essential data structure that helps in calculating different performance measures such as precision, accuracy, recall, and sensitivity of classification technique on some data.

Table 1 Confusion Matrix

	Negative	Positive
Negative	TN (True Negative)	FN (False Negative)
Positive	FP (False Positive)	TP (True Positive)

36

Table 1 provides a sample confusion matrix table and Eq. 28-31 illustrates the formulas to calculate different performance measures.

$$Accuracy = \frac{TN+TP}{TP+TN+FP+FN} \dots\dots\dots\dots\dots\dots\dots\dots\dots\dots\dots\dots\dots\dots\dots\dots$$
(28)

$$False\ Positive\ Rate = \frac{FP}{TN+FP} \dots\dots\dots\dots\dots\dots\dots\dots\dots\dots\dots\dots\dots (29)$$

$$Precision = \frac{TP}{FP+TP} \dots\dots\dots\dots\dots\dots\dots\dots\dots\dots\dots\dots\dots\dots (30)$$

$$Sensitivity = \frac{TP}{FN+TP} \dots\dots\dots\dots\dots\dots\dots\dots\dots\dots\dots\dots\dots\dots (31)$$

3.3 Data Collection

3.3.1 Description of dataset for Result No. 1, 2 3

The traffic and road accident data is obtained from the online data source for Leeds UK [70]. This data set comprises 13062 accident that occurred during 2011 to 2015. Initial preprocessing of the data results in 11 attributes that found to be suitable for further analysis. The attributes selected for analysis are a number of vehicles, time of the accident, road surface, weather conditions, lightening conditions, casualty class, sex of casualty, age, type of vehicle, day and month of the accident. The accident data is illustrated in Table 2.

Table 2 Road Accident Attribute Description

S. No.	Attribute	Code	Value	Total	Casualty Class		
					Driver	Passenger	Pedestrian
1.	No. of vehicles	1	1 vehicle	3334	763	817	753
		2	2 vehicle	7991	5676	2215	99
		3+	>3 vehicle	5214	1218	510	10
2.	Time	T1	[0-4]	630	269	250	110
		T2	[4-8]	903	698	133	71
		T3	[6-12]	2720	1701	644	374
		T4	[12-16]	3342	1812	1027	502
		T5	[16-20]	3976	2387	990	598
		T6	[20-24]	1496	790	498	207
3.	Road Surface	OTR	Other	106	62	30	13
		DR	Dry	9828	5687	2695	1445
		WT	Wet	3063	1858	803	401

		SNW	Snow	157	101	39	16
		FLD	Flood	17	11	5	0
4.	Lightening Condition	DLGT	Day Light	9020	5422	2348	1249
		NLGT	No Light	1446	858	389	198
		SLGT	Street Light	2598	1377	805	415
5.	Weather Condition	CLR	Clear	11584	6770	3140	1666
		FG	Fog	37	26	7	3
		SNY	Snowy	63	41	15	6
		RNY	Rainy	1276	751	350	174
6.	Casualty Class	DR	Driver		7657	0	0
		PSG	Passenger		0	3542	0
		PDT	Pedestrian		0	0	1862
7.	Sex of Casualty	M	Male	7758	5223	1460	1074
		F	Female	5305	2434	2082	788
8.	Age	Minor	<18 years	1976	454	855	667
		Youth	18-30 years	4267	2646	1158	462
		Adult	30-60 years	4254	3152	742	359
		Senior	>60 years	2567	1405	787	374
9.	Type of Vehicle	BS	Bus	842	52	687	102
		CR	Car	9208	4959	2692	1556
		GDV	Goods Vehicle	449	245	86	117
		BCL	Bicycle	1512	1476	11	24
		PTV	PTWW	977	876	48	52
		OTR	Other	79	49	18	11
10.	Day	WKD	Weekday	9884	5980	2499	1404
		WND	Weekend	3179	1677	1043	458
11.	Month	Q1	Jan-March	3017	1731	803	482
		Q2	April-June	3220	1887	907	425
		Q3	Jul-Sep	3376	2021	948	406
		Q4	Oct-Dec	3452	2018	884	549

3.3.2 Description of dataset for Result No. 4

The traffic accident data set was obtained from police records of Muzzafarnagar district, Uttar Pradesh. A total of 2300 accident records were selected for analysis. The dataset consists of information about road accident type, the age of the victim, the location of accidents, time and date of accidents, victim gender, type of vehicle etc. The brief distribution of road accidents is given in Table 3.

Table 3 Road Accident Attribute Description

S. No.	Attribute	Attribute Values	Code	Total
1.	Number of Victims NOV	1 victim	1	1200
		2 victim	2	855
		3 or more victim	+2	245
2.	Age of victim: AOV	0-18 years	CHD	305
		18-30 years	YNG	722
		30-50 years	ADU	815
		50 or more years	SNR	458
3.	Gender: GEN	Male	M	1589
		Female	F	711
4.	Time of day: TOD	[0-6]	T1	155
		[6-12]	T2	660
		[12-18]	T3	626
		[18-24]	T4	859
5.	Month: MON	Jan-Mar	Q1	611
		Apr-Jun	Q2	468
		Jul-Sep	Q3	590
		Oct-Dec	Q4	631
6.	Lighting condition: LIG	Day Light	DLT	1180
		Dusk	DUS	365
		Road Light	RLT	270
		No Light	NLT	485
7.	Roadway Feature: ROF	Intersection	INT	985
		Slope	SLP	320
		Curve	CUR	458
		Straight	STR	537
8.	Road Type: ROT	Highway	HIW	1459
		Local	LOC	841
9.	Accident Severity: ASV	Killed or Severe	KSI	712
		Slight Injury	SI	1588
10.	Surrounding Area: SUA	Agriculture Land	AGL	898
		Commercial	MAR	846
		Residential	COL	556
11.	Day of Week	Weekday	WDAY	1227
		Weekend	WEND	1073

3.3.3 Description of dataset for Result No. 5

Airplane crash data obtained from Federal Aviation Administration, USA [71]. This dataset contains all airplane crashes between "1908 - 2016". The dataset contained few attributes like Date, Time, Location, Operator, Flight, Route, Type, Registration, Aboard, Fatalities, Ground, and Summary. We separated summary column from this dataset because the summary column was totally text and our aim was to work on text analysis.

Chapter 4

ANALYSIS AND RESULTS

4.1 Introduction

There are several machine learning approaches has been implemented to achieve accuracy and determine the most occurrence factor involved in an accident. Results are divided into 5 sections.

4.2 Result No. 1 (Road-user Specific Analysis of Traffic Accident using Data Mining Techniques)

4.2.1 Classification Analysis

Several approaches have been utilized to classify this bunch of dataset on the basis of casualty class using SVM (support vector machine), Naïve bays and Decision tree. The classification accuracy achieved is shown in Fig 3. It can be seen that decision tree obtained the highest accuracy of 70.7% in comparison to other two classifiers.

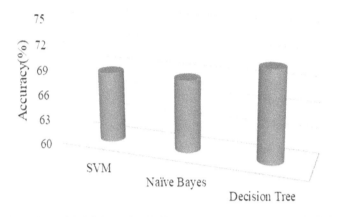

Figure 3 Classification accuracy of different classifiers on accident data

4.2.2 Classification followed by clustering of accident

In this analysis, two clustering techniques have been utilized which are SOM (Self-organizing map) and K-modes techniques. Achieved result is better by using k-modes as compared to SOM technique and therefore demonstrating the performance of classifiers on clusters attained by k-modes only.

a. Performance evaluation of SVM

In this study, SVM is applied to classify dataset on the basis of casualty class and this classifier classified data into 3 classes. The output of this classifier are determined on the basis of their precision, recall, error rate and other factors and enhanced achieved accuracy which is *75.5838 %* and it's increased approximately 7% and it is better than earlier analyzed dataset without clustering. Table 4 provides the performance of SVM on clusters attained from k-modes.

Table 4 Performance of SVM

Rate of error= 0.1628							
Predicted values				**Confusion Matrix**			
Class	Precision	Recall	TPR	FPR	Class	DR	PSG	PDT
DR	0.779	0.909	0.90	0.36	DR	6958	153	546
PSG	0.824	0.375	0.37	0.03	PSG	1828	1330	384
PDT	0.630	0.851	0.85	0.083	PDT	146	132	1584

b. Performance evaluation of Naïve Bayes

In this study, Naïve Bays applied to classify dataset on the basis of casualty class and this classifier classified dataset into 3 classes. Here again, it can be seen that output is determined on the basis of precision, recall, error, error rate, TPR and other various factors which play a really important role. Enhanced accuracy reached to 76.4583% which is approximately better than earlier without clustering which was 68.5375%. Table 5 provides the performance of Naïve Bayes on clusters attained from k-modes.

Table 5 Performance of Naive Bayes

Rate of error=0.2352							
Predicted values				**Confusion Matrix**			
Class	Precision	Recall	TPR	FPR	Class	DR	PSG	PDT
DR	0.788	0.86	0.86	0.33	DR	6649	515	493
PSG	0.697	0.43	0.43	0.07	PSG	1624	1535	383
PDT	0.742	0.828	0.828	0.078	PDT	170	151	1541

c. Performance evaluation of Decision Tree

In this study, Decision Tree classifier has been used which improved the accuracy better than earlier without clustering. Achieved accuracy 81 %which is better than earlier. Table 6 provides the performance of decision tree on clusters attained from k-modes.

Table 6 Performance of Decision Tree

Rate of error=0.1628							
Predicted values				**Confusion Matrix**			
Class	Precision	Recall	TPR	FPR	Class	DR	PSG	PDT
DR	0.784	0.893	0.893	0.348	DR	6841	422	394
PSG	0.724	0.457	0.457	0.065	PSG	1649	1620	273
PDT	0.683	0.770	0.770	0.060	PDT	231	197	1434

4.2.3 Analysis

Achieved error rate, precision, TPR (True positive rate), FPR (False positive rate), Precision, recall for every classification techniques as shown in given tables and also achieved different confusion matrix for different classification techniques. It can be seen the performance of different classifier techniques by the help of confusion matrix.

Here in the next table, it is shown the overall accuracy of analysis with clustering with the help of Table 4-6 and as it can be observed from these tables classification accuracy increased for each classification technique after doing clustering.

Fig 4 illustrates the classification accuracy of SVM, Naïve Bayes and decision tree on clusters obtained from k-modes and SOM. It can be seen that classification accuracy is better for clusters obtained from k-modes clustering rather than obtained from SOM. It can be concluded that k-modes clustering technique provides better clustering than SOM on data with categorical road accident attributes.

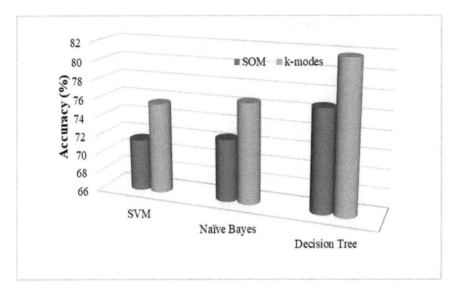

Figure 4 Classification accuracy on clusters obtained from k-modes and SOM

This result is part of my research article [24].

4.3 Result No. 2 (Performance Evaluation of Lazy, Decision Tree Classifier and Multilayer Perceptron on Traffic Accident Analysis)

4.3.1 Direct Classification Analysis

There are different approaches used to classifying this bunch of dataset on the basis of casualty class. A classifier which are Decision Tree, Lazy classifier, and Multilayer Perceptron. It can be seen the result at some level from Table 7.

Table 7 Direct classified Accuracy

Classifiers	Accuracy
Lazy classifier(K-Star)	67.7324%
Lazy classifier (IBK)	68.5634%
Decision Tree	70.7566%
Multilayer perceptron	69.3031%

It can be seen the table 7 that achieved accuracy is achieved directly without clustering and then further there are different clustering techniques used such as Hierarchical clustering and K-modes.

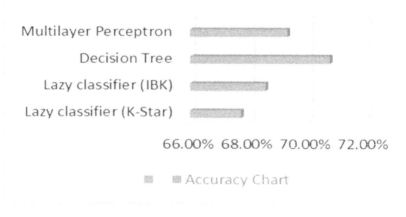

Figure 5 Direct classified Accuracy

4.3.2 Classification followed by clustering techniques

In this analysis, two clustering approaches have been implemented which are Hierarchical and K-modes techniques, Later dataset are divided into 9 clusters. Achieved accuracy is better by using Hierarchical as compared to K-modes techniques.

a. Lazy Classifier Output

K-Star: In this, classified result increased from 67.7324 % to 82.352%. It's sharp improvement in the result after clustering

Table 8 Detailed Accuracy of K-Star by Class

TP Rate	FP Rate	Precision	Recall	F-Measure	MCC	ROC Area	PRC Area	Class
0.956	0.320	0.809	0.956	0.876	0.679	0.928	0.947	Driver
0.529	0.029	0.873	0.529	0.659	0.600	0.917	0.824	Passenger
0.839	0.027	0.837	0.839	0.838	0.811	0.981	0.906	Pedestrian

IBK: In this, classified result increased from 68.5634% to 84.4729%. It's sharp improvement in the result after clustering.

Table 9 Detailed Accuracy of IBK by Class

TP Rate	FP Rate	Precision	Recall	F-Measure	MCC	ROC Area	PRC Area	Class
0.945	0.254	0.840	0.945	0.890	0.717	0.950	0.964	Driver
0.644	0.048	0.833	0.644	0.726	0.651	0.940	0.867	Passenger
0.816	0.018	0.884	0.816	0.849	0.826	0.990	0.946	Pedestrian

b. Decision Tree Output

In this study, Decision Tree classifier has been used which improved the accuracy better than earlier without clustering. It can be seen that achieved accuracy 84.4575 % which is almost 15 % more than without clustering.

Table 10 Detailed Accuracy of Decision Tree by Class

TP Rate	FP Rate	Precision	Recall	F-Measure	MCC	ROC Area	PRC Area	Class
0.922	0.220	0.856	0.922	0.888	0.717	0.946	0.961	Driver
0.665	0.057	0.814	0.665	0.732	0.652	0.936	0.861	Passenger
0.868	0.027	0.841	0.868	0.855	0.830	0.988	0.939	Pedestrian

c. Multilayer Perceptron Output

In this study, accuracy increased from 69.3031% to 78.8301% after using clustering technique.

Table 11 Detailed Accuracy of Multilayer Perceptron by Class

TP Rate	FP Rate	Precision	Recall	F-Measure	MCC	ROC Area	PRC Area	Class
0.929	0.338	0.796	0.929	0.857	0.627	0.892	0.916	Driver
0.452	0.036	0.824	0.452	0.584	0.520	0.855	0.720	Passenger
0.849	0.053	0.726	0.849	0.783	0.746	0.955	0.818	Pedestrian

4.3.3 Analysis

Achieved error rate, precision, TPR (True positive rate), FPR (False positive rate), Precision, recall for every classification techniques as shown in given tables and also achieved different confusion matrix for different classification techniques. It can be seen the performance of different classifier techniques by the help of confusion matrix.

Here in the next table, it is shown the overall accuracy of analysis with clustering with the help of table 12, as it can be compared this table from the previous table that accuracy increased in each classification techniques after doing clustering.

Table 12 Classified Accuracy followed by Clustering

Classifiers	Accuracy
Lazy classifier (K-Star)	82.352%
Lazy classifier (IBK)	84.4729%
Decision Tree	84.4575%
Multilayer perceptron	78.8301%

It can be seen accuracy level of table 12 in given figure 6 with the help of chart and can be seen from the chart that it's improved after doing clustering in accuracy chart also

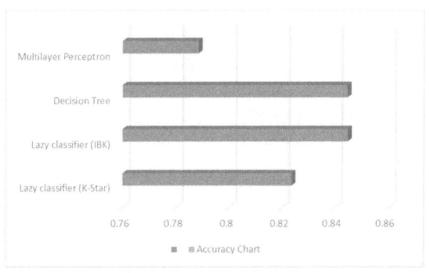

Figure 6 Accuracy after clustering

As it can be seen from Table 7 and 12 that accuracy level increased after clustering. It is shown comparison chart in fig. 7 without clustering and with clustering.

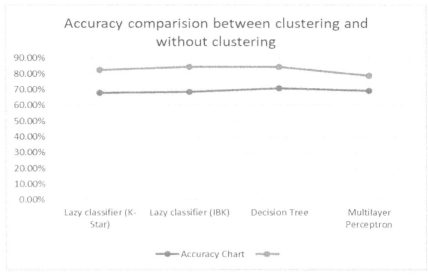

Figure 7 Compared accuracy chart with clustering and without clustering

This result is part of my research article [23].

4.4 Result No. 3 (A Conjoint Analysis of Road Accident Data using K-modes clustering and Bayesian Networks)

This section presents the experimental analysis and discussion on results. Initially, data preprocessing is performed on the road accident data to give it a proper shape required for analysis. Several attributes are transformed into the suitable form using data transformation methods.

4.4.1 Cluster Analysis

After data selection and data preprocessing, the selected data is used for cluster analysis using k-modes clustering algorithm. The number of clusters for the k-modes algorithm is determined by observing the BIC values for different cluster models. Fig 8 illustrates the cluster selection using BIC values.

Based on fact mentioned in previous studies [3, 76], a cluster model with 4 clusters is selected. Further, the k-modes technique is applied on the data and the four cluster obtained. The description of these four clusters is given in Table 13.

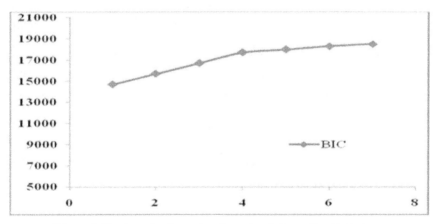

Figure 8 Cluster selection using Bayesian Information Criteria

Table 13 Cluster description

Cluster Id	Description	No. of accidents	Size (%)
C1	Two wheeler accidents in bad weather	196	15
C2	Other accidents in bad weather	299	24
C3	Other accident in clear weather	247	20
C4	Two wheeler accidents in bad weather	504	41

Table 14 Bayesian network performance on each cluster and whole dataset

Subset	Accuracy	Sensitivity	Specificity	HMSS	ROC
C1	0.88	0.68	0.91	0.778	0.776
C2	0.85	0.59	0.94	0.724	0.874
C3	0.78	0.40	0.93	0.559	0.796
C4	0.85	0.78	0.86	0.818	0.708
WD	0.84	0.59	0.90	0.712	0.856

4.4.2 Performance Evaluation of Bayesian Network

Further, Bayesian Networks (BNs) are used to investigate the responsible circumstances that lend to accident severity. Therefore, several BNs were built for every cluster and the whole data set.

The aim of this study is to identify if some new findings are thereafter performing a conjoint analysis (k-modes and BN). Further, these BNs that were built for 4 clusters and whole data set were compared using performance indicators and complexity to validate the goodness of model fitting. Table 14 illustrates the accuracy, sensitivity, specificity and HMSS and ROC for each cluster and whole data (WD).

4.4.3 Analysis

It can be seen from Table 14 that minimum accuracy is attained in C3 and the highest accuracy is attained in C1. As the accident data was imbalanced data, ROC values are also taken into consideration. The ROC values indicate that performance of classification is better in C2 whereas, in other clusters, the ROC values are lower than the ROC value of WD. It simply indicates that although more accuracy can achieve as a result of clustering process but is the data is of imbalanced nature, it is not guaranteed that efficient classification results can be achieved.

This result is part of my research article [25].

4.5 Result No. 4 (Augmenting Classifiers Performance through Clustering: A Comparative Study on Road Accident Data)

4.5.1 Cluster Analysis

The first step of our analysis is associated with identification of an appropriate number of clusters to be formed. We used R statistical software to serve this purpose. The different AIC, BIC, CAIC values are calculated for different cluster models. Also, Gap statistic curve was plotted against different cluster models along with an elbow plot. The most essential and good achievement is that all cluster selection criteria agreed on the same cluster value i.e. k=2. AIC, BIC and CAIC graphs (Fig 9) shows that there is no further improvement in their values after cluster value 2. Similarly, elbow plot (Fig 10) indicates that knee curve exists at cluster number 2 and Gap statistic curve (Fig 11 & 13) illustrates that maximum gap exists at cluster position 2. Hence, I have selected the cluster number 2 to form clusters out of the data.

Further, performed cluster analysis using LCC, k-modes and BIRCH techniques to obtain the desired number of clusters from the data. It is found that k-modes clustering takes comparatively less time to compute different clusters than LCC and BIRCH techniques. The distribution of data into clusters attained from above-mentioned techniques are given in Table 15. It is clear from the Table 15 that the size of the clusters obtained from LCC, k-modes, and BIRCH are not similar. Clearly, the reason lies within the different mechanism of creating clusters of each technique. Our next task is to investigate the performance of NB, SVM and RF techniques to predict the severity of traffic accidents.

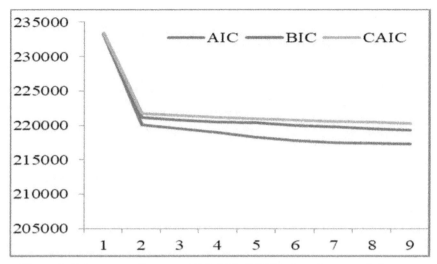

Figure 9: Information Criterion (AIC, BIC, CAIC) values for several cluster models

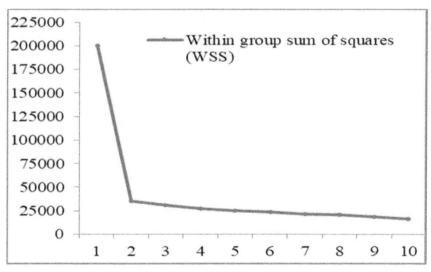

Figure 10 Elbow plot

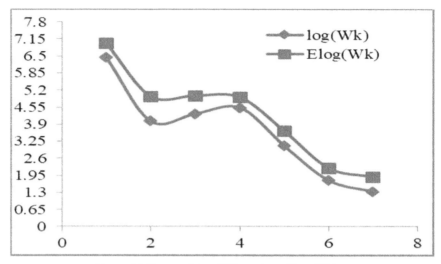

Figure 11 Expected log (Wk) vs Actual log (Wk)

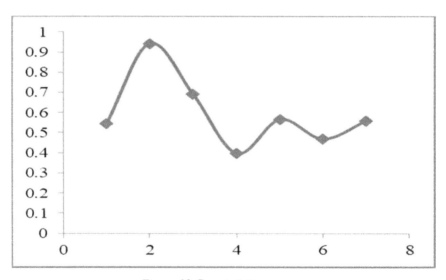

Figure 12 Gap statistic curve

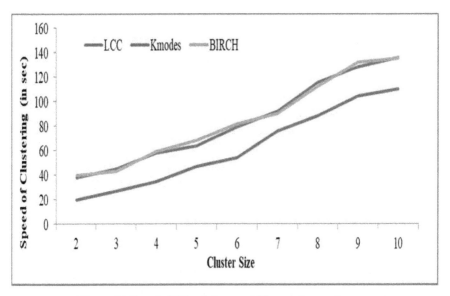

Figure 13 Speed of Clustering on different cluster sizes

Table 15 Cluster wise distribution of road accidents for each clustering technique

	LCC		K-modes		BIRCH	
	C1	C2	C1	C2	C1	C2
KSI	320	392	344	368	300	412
SI	765	823	716	872	784	804
Total	1085	1215	1060	1240	1084	1216

4.5.2 Classification Analysis

The WEKA tool and R language are used to perform the classification using NB, SVM and RF model on the clusters attained from LCC, k-modes and BIRCH technique. The performance of the three classification model is illustrated in Table 16 for every of the clustering techniques and for entire data without clustering.

Table 16 Classification accuracy of different classifiers

S. No.	Clustering technique	Classification Accuracy (%)		
		NB	SVM	RF
1	LCC	79%	72%	81%
2	K-modes	76.4%	70%	79.95%
3	BIRCH	68.3%	64%	78.5%
4	Without clustering (Whole data)	70%	68%	79%

4.5.3 Analysis

Table 16 illustrates the performance of NB, SVM and RF models on the classification of traffic and road accident data with or without clustering. It is clear that classification accuracy of all techniques is highest after clustering of data using LCC technique. Classification accuracy also improved after clustering with k-modes technique but slightly decreased after clustering using BIRCH technique. It is clear that the method used by BIRCH clustering is not able to create good clusters as compared to other two clustering approaches. On the other part, it can be seen that cluster computation speed of K-modes clustering method is better than LCC and BIRCH clustering. Therefore, on the basis of computation speed, K-modes clustering are the best choice among the three available techniques whereas on the basis of clustered data, LCC provides better clusters that provide better classification and it has been verified using three popular techniques NB, SVM and RF.

This analysis clearly indicates that LCC clustering wins the competition on road accident data as it generates clusters to achieve the maximum classification accuracy but K-modes wins the competition if we only consider the computation efficiency of clustering algorithms.

This result is part of my research article [26].

4.5 Result No. 5 (Analysis of Airplane crash by utilizing Text Mining Techniques)

4.5.1 Cluster Analysis

Hierarchical clustering, Self-Organizing Map has been utilized and achieved the approximately same type of clusters for both approaches. To identify recurrence related words, initially, process a separation network in view of our lessened Document-Term Matrix, then applied hierarchical clustering and Self-Organizing Map to achieve a group of clustered words. It is divided into 18 clusters. Here, achieved group which is produced by clustering.

- *conditions, weather*
- *landing*
- *emergency, failed, loss, lost, power, shortly*
- *altitude, mountain*
- *accident, pilots, terrain*
- *continued, flames, heavy, hit, maintain, rain, sea, stalled, turn, vfr, visibility*
- *pilot*
- *failure*
- *airport, fire, fuel*
- *takeoff*
- *air, feet, miles, poor, route*
- *crew*
- *attempting, land*
- *area, descent, error, flying, fog, high, improper, low, minutes, short, trees*
- *approach, runway*
- *engine*
- *left, right, wing*
- *cargo, control, ground, struck, taking*

By plotting cluster through the help of "factoextra" package, it can be visualize the clusters that how they are a far from each other.

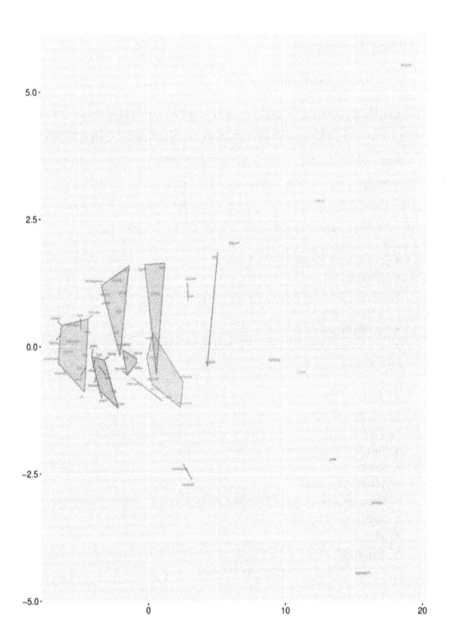

Figure 14 Visualization of clusters

From figure no 14, it can be seen some group of words which might be situation or reason of plane crashed. These words are:

- *Incorrect altitude*
- *Engine*
- *Approach of runway*
- *Pilot*
- *Poor visibility and weather condition*

4.5.2 Association Rule Mining

By using association rule mining, it can be seen most occurrence terms and their association with other terms as well. It is shown in figure no.15 by plotting most occurrence 25 terms. All these terms are part of those 18 clusters but we achieved here their occurrence associated with each other.

Contingency of top 25 most frequent terms

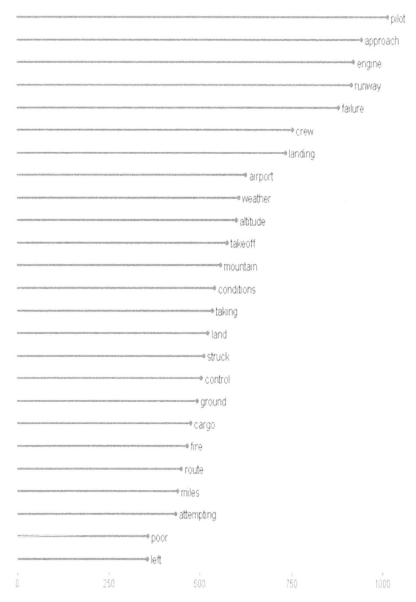

Figure 15 Most Frequent Terms

There are few terms which have a high impact on crashes such as:

- *Runway:* associated to the approach stage
- *Approach:* this depict that accident frequently happened at runway approach stage
- *Failure:* This is nonspecific to extract conclusion.
- *Engine:* This one is most common reason for crashes
- *Pilot:* This one is a nonspecific term which is difficult to determine the cause of pilot or something else.

To get inside more and understand reason more properly, it is tried to find which terms are more associated with those top 25 frequently occurrence terms. It has been calculated most 5 terms which have correlation limit higher than 0.18 because this threshold value is empirical and it has been tested on different values like 0.15, 0.17, 0.18, 0.19, 0.20, 0.21 but 0.18 provided a correct number of correlated words for every term.

4.5.3 Analysis

Now it can be seen more precisely about the cause which is discussed here:

- ***Runway:*** This term is associated with such words like 'end', 'short' and 'overran'. That might be during the stage of landing or takeoff.
- ***Approach:*** This term is associated with such words like 'missed', 'instruments', 'ils', 'visual'. This seems like crashes happened because of minimum visibility and mistake during reading instruments.
- ***Failure:*** We achieved some more precise relation here which is explaining that reason would be a procedure, pilot, system failure or maintenance.
- ***Engine:*** This is suggesting that loss of power or engine shut down would because of crash

- ***Conditions and Weather:*** This also suggest that visibility was also reason for crashes in bad weathers
- ***Pilot:*** We achieved in our calculation that 'error' is associated term so 60 % of accident happened because of error of pilots

This result is part of my research article [27].

Chapter 5

CONCLUSION AND RECOMMENDATIONS

In this study, there are several data mining approaches has been performed to analyze accident dataset by using different clustering techniques such as SOM (Self Organizing Map), K-modes, Hierarchical clustering, latent class clustering (LCC), BIRCH clustering as well as classification techniques which are Support Vector Machine (SVM), Naïve Bays, Decision Tree (Random Forest, J-48 etc.), Multilayer Perceptron, Lazy Classifier (K-star and IBK), Bayesian Network to find pattern on road user specific and achieved better accuracy followed by using clustering techniques. In this, classifier accuracy is enhanced by this way on the basis of casualty class so it can be seen clearly that what factors affect (like most accidents happened between 12:00-20:00 and driver was involved in most of the cases, Dry road surface, day lightening condition, clear weather condition, most of them are youth and adult, mostly car involved in accident, weekday, Male etc.) and who is involved more in an accident between the driver, passenger or pedestrian. From result no. 1, k-modes provided better clustering results as compared to SOM and classification accuracy of SVM, Naïve Bays, and Decision Tree is found better on clusters attained from k-modes. It indicates that clustering certainly enhance the classification accuracy of classifiers and k-modes clustering would be a better option to cluster road accident data with categorical attributes. Result no. 2 is improved version of result no.1 where different approaches have been utilized to improve the accuracy. Hierarchical clustering provided the better result as compared to k-mode clustering.

The motivation of these study is to validate the performance of classification before and after clustering techniques. From result no.3, K-modes clustering was utilized to cluster dataset into 4 homogeneous groups and then later, this cluster and whole dataset were analyzed by using Bayesian Network. Different Bayesian Networks are built for each cluster and the entire data. Further, these Bayesian Networks are evaluated on the basis of performance indicators. The result indicates the classification accuracy is slightly improved as a result of clustering process but the ROC values are slightly decreased for some clusters. This indicates that performance of the classifier in terms of accuracy is biased towards one class value which has an approximately large number of instances.

This study provides a comparative study on the performance of three clustering techniques LCC, k-modes and BIRCH on a traffic accident data in Indian district. From result no. 4, the motive of this study to identify which one of the above three techniques generate efficient clusters for classification purpose. Diverse cluster selection criteria are used to locate the appropriate number of clusters from the data. All used criteria agreed on the same number of clusters i.e. k=2. We then applied three popular classification techniques NB, SVM, and RF on the clusters obtained from the previously mentioned clustering techniques. The results showed that LCC clustering generated better clusters in comparison to other two techniques and achieves the maximum classification accuracy by NB, SVM, and RF technique. It has been also evaluated the computational performance of the three clustering techniques on a different number of cluster models. It is found that k-modes provide better computation speed than other two techniques to generate a different number of clusters.

From the study of result no.5, analyzed airplane crash dataset. This dataset contains all accident happened between "1908 - 2016". There are few approaches utilized such as Self-Organizing Map (SOM), hierarchical clustering technique and association rule to recognize the association between most frequent terms. There is some most common cause of accidents achieved associated with Engine, Failure, Weather condition, Pilot, Approach, and

Runway etc. Crashes might be deteriorated in near future if cause would be taken into consideration.

The study can be useful for the authors who wish to select a clustering algorithm to generate homogeneous segments out of accident data based on computation speed or better clusters for classification.

References:

1. Han, J. and Kamber, M., Data mining: concepts and techniques, Academic Press, ISBN 1- 55860-489-8.
2. Data mining: practical machine learning tools and techniques.—3rd ed. /Ian H. Witten, Frank Eibe, Mark A. Hall.
3. Depaire B, Wets G, Vanhoof K. Traffic accident segmentation by means of latent class clustering. Accid Anal Prev.2008;40(4):1257–66.
4. Miaou SP. The Relationship between truck accidents and geometric design of road sections-poisson versus negative binomial regressions. Accid Anal Prev. 1994;26(4):471–82.
5. Miaou SP, Lum H. Modeling vehicle accidents and highway geometric design relationships. Accid Anal Prev. 1993;25(6):689–709.
6. Ma J, Kockelman K. Crash frequency and severity modeling using clustered data from Washington state. In: IEEE intelligent transportation systems conference. Toronto; 2006.
7. Savolainen P, Mannering F, Lord D, Quddus M. The statistical analysis of highway crash-injury severities: a review and assessment of methodological alternatives. Accid Anal Prev. 2011;43(5):1666–76.
8. Geurts K, Wets G, Brijs T, Vanhoof K (2003) Profiling of high-frequency accident locations by use of association rules. Transp Res Rec. doi:10.3141/1840-14.
9. Jonas Poelmans, Sergei O. Kuznetsov, Dmitry I. Ignatov, Guido Dedene, Formal Concept Analysis in knowledge processing: A survey on models and techniques. In: Expert Systems with Applications, Vol. 40. No. 16, pp. 6601-6623, 2013.
10. Barai S (2003) Data mining application in transportation engineering, Transport, vol. 18, pp. 216–223. doi:10.1080/16483840.2003. 10414100.
11. Berry, Michael J. A. and Linoff. G. S. (1997). Data mining techniques: for marketing, sales, and customer relationship management / Michael J.A. Berry, Gordon Linoff 2nd ed.
12. Mussone, L., Ferrari, A. and Oneta, M. An analysis of urban collisions using an artificial intelligence model. Accid Anal Prev 1999, vol. 31, pp. 705-718.
13. Kumar, S. and Toshniwal, D. A data mining framework to analyze road accident data. Journal of Big Data, vol. 2, No. 26, pp. 1-18.
14. Chang, L.Y. and Chen, W.C. Data mining of tree based models to analyze freeway accident frequency. J Saf Res Elsevier. 2005; vol. 36.
15. Kohavi, Ron (1995). "A study of cross-validation and bootstrap for accuracy estimation and model selection". Proceedings of the Fourteenth

International Joint Conference on Artificial Intelligence (San Mateo, CA: Morgan Kaufmann) 2 (12): 1137–1143.

16. Matthews, B.W. Comparison of the predicted and observed secondary structure of T4 phage lysozyme". Biochimica et Biophysica Acta (BBA) - Protein Structure, 1975, 405 (2): 442–451.

17. Fawcett, Tom (2006). "An Introduction to ROC Analysis". Pattern Recognition Letters, 2006, 27 (8): 861 – 874.

18. A. Montella, M. Aria, A. D'Ambrosio, F. Mauriello, Data mining techniques for exploratory analysis of pedestrian crashes, Transportation Research Record, 2237, 2011, pp. 107–116.

19. Karlaftis M, Tarko A (1998) Heterogeneity considerations in accident modeling. Accid Anal Prev 30(4):425–433.

20. Kumar S, Toshniwal D (2015) A data mining framework to analyze road accident data. J Big Data 2(1):1–18. doi:10.1186/s40537-015-0035-y

21. Ulfarsson GF, Mannering FL (2004) Difference in male and female injury severities in sport-utility vehicle, minivan, pickup and passenger car accidents. Accid Anal Prev 36(2):135–147.

22. Savolainen P, Mannering F (2007) Probabilistic models of motorcyclists' injury severities in single- and multi-vehicle crashes. Accid Anal Prev 39(5):955–963.

23. Tiwari, Prayag, Huy Dao, and Gia Nhu Nguyen. "Performance Evaluation of Lazy, Decision Tree Classifier and Multilayer Perceptron on Traffic Accident Analysis." Informatica 41.1 (2017).

24. Tiwari, Prayag, Sachin Kumar, and Denis Kalitin. "Road-User Specific Analysis of Traffic Accident Using Data Mining Techniques." International Conference on Computational Intelligence, Communications, and Business Analytics. Springer, Singapore, 2017.

25. K Sachin, Shemwal V.B., Tiwari P., Solanki V., K Denis. "A Conjoint Analysis of Road Accident Data using K-modes clustering and Bayesian Networks," Annals of Computer Science and Information System, Volume 10, 53-56.

26. Tiwari P., Kumar S., Shemwal V.B , Sharma B., Kalitin D., Augmenting Classifiers Performance through Clustering: A Comparative Study on Road Accident Data- Accepted for publication in International Journal of Information Retrieval Research.

27. Tiwari P., Nguyen G.N., Prasad M., Pratama M., Ashour A.S., Dey N., Analysis of Airplane crash by utilizing Text Mining Techniques- under review process in Acta Informatica.

28. P. Tiwari, "Improvement of ETL through integration of query cache and scripting method," 2016 International Conference on Data Science and

Engineering (ICDSE), Cochin, India, 2016, pp. 1-5. doi:10.1109/ICDSE.2016.7823935.

29. P. Tiwari, "Advanced ETL (AETL) by integration of PERL and scripting method," 2016 International Conference on Inventive Computation Technologies (ICICT), Coimbatore, India,2016,pp.1-5.doi:10.1109/INVENTIVE.2016.7830102.

30. P. Tiwari, S. Kumar, A.C. Mishra, V. Kumar, B. Terfa, "Improved Performance of Data Warehouse," International Conference on Inventive Communication and Computational Technologies (ICICCT-2017), Coimbatore, 10-11 March 2017. Proceeding will be published IEEE-Xplore.

31. Tiwari P., Nguyen G.N., Kumar S., Yadav P., Ashour A.S., Dey N., Sentiment Analysis based on Russian and English Review Dataset-accepted in Statistical Analysis and Data Mining: The ASA Data Science Journal.

32. Tiwari, P., Mishra, B. K., Kumar, S., & Kumar, V. (2017). Implementation of n-gram Methodology for Rotten Tomatoes Review Dataset Sentiment Analysis. International Journal of Knowledge Discovery in Bioinformatics (IJKDB), 7(1), 30-41. doi:10.4018/IJKDB.2017010103

33. Prayag Tiwari. Article: Comparative Analysis of Big Data. International Journal of Computer Applications 140(7):24-29, April 2016. Published by Foundation of Computer Science (FCS), NY, USA.

34. Tiwari P, Mishra AC, Jha AK (2016) Case Study as a Method for Scope Definition. Arabian J Bus Manag Review S1:002

35. V. Kumar, D. Kalitin, P. Tiwari, "Unsupervised Learning Dimensionality Reduction Algorithm PCA For Face Recognition," International Conference on Computing Communication and Automations (ICCCA)" proceeding will be published in IEEE-Xplore.

36. Kumar V, Yadav P, Samadhiya A, Jain A, Tiwari P, Comparative Performance Analysis of Image De-noising Techniques, International Conference on Innovations in Engineering and Technology(ICIET)Bangkok,Thailand2013,http://dx.doi.org/10.15242/II E.E1213576.

37. Kumar, S and Toshniwal, D. (2016a) Analysis of road accident counts using hierarchical clustering and cophenetic correlation coefficient (CPCC). Journal of Big Data, 3, 13:1-11.

38. Kumar, S. and Toshniwal, D. (2016b) A novel framework to analyze road accident time series data. Journal of Big Data, 3, 8:1-11

39. Kumar S, Toshniwal D. (2015b) Analysing road accident data using association rule mining. Proceedings in IEEE International Conference on Computing, Communication and Security held in Mauritius. India: IEEE Xplore; 4-6 Dec, 2015.

40. Kumar S and Toshniwal D (2017) Severity Analysis of Powered Two Wheeler Traffic Accidents in Uttarakhand, India, European Transport Research Review, Springer, vol. 9 (2), pp. 1-10.

41. Kumar S, Toshniwal D and Parida M. (2016d) A comparative analysis of heterogeneity in road accident data using data mining techniques. Evolving Systems. Springer. 2016; DOI: 10.1007/s12530-016-9165-5.

42. Jones B, Janssen L, and Mannering F (1991) Analysis of the Frequency and Durationof Freeway Accidents in Seattle, Accident Analysis and Prevention, Elsevier, vol. 23.

43. Poch M, and Mannering F (1996) Negative Binomial Analysis of Intersection-Accident Frequencies, Journal of Transportation Engineering, vol. 122.

44. Ma J, Kockelman K. (2006). Crash frequency, and severity modeling using clustered data from Washington state. In: IEEE Intelligent Transportation Systems Conference. Toronto Canadá; 2006.

45. Kwon OH, Rhee W, Yoon Y (2015) Application of classification algorithms for analysis of road safety risk factor dependencies. Accid Anal Prev, vol. 75, pp. 1–15. doi:10.1016/j.aap.2014.11.005.

46. Sohn S.Y., Lee S. H., Data fusion, ensemble and clustering to improve the classification accuracy for the severity of road traffic accidents in Korea, Safety Science, vol. 41(1), pp. 1-14.

47. Tibebe B. T., Abraham A., Grosan C., Rule mining and classification of road traffic accidents using adaptive regression trees , I. J. of simulation vol. 6, 10.

48. M. Kaytoue, S.O. Kuznetsov, A. Napoli, S. Duplessis, Mining gene expression data with pattern structures in formal concept analysis. Information Sciences, Volume 181, Issue 10, 15 May 2011, pp. 1989-2001, Information Science, Special Issue on Information Engineering Applications Based on Lattices, Elsevier, New York, 2011.

49. Sergei O. Kuznetsov, Fitting Pattern Structures to Knowledge Discovery in Big Data. In: Cellier, Peggy; Distel, Felix; Ganter, Bernhard, Eds., Proc. 11th International Conference on Formal Concept Analysis (ICFCA 2013), Lecture Notes in Artificial Intelligence (Springer), Vol. 7880, pp. 254–266, 2013.

50. Sergei O. Kuznetsov, Jonas Poelmans, Knowledge representation and processing with formal concept analysis. In: Wiley Interdisciplinary

Reviews: Data Mining and Knowledge Discovery, Vol.3 (3), pp. 200-215, 2013.

51. Christopher, AB Arockia, and S. Appavu alias Balamurugan. "Prediction of warning level in aircraft accidents using data mining techniques." The Aeronautical Journal 118.1206 (2014): 935-952.

52. Arockia Christopher A.B., Appavu alias Balamurugan S. (2014) Prediction of Warning Level in Aircraft Accidents using Classification Techniques: An Empirical Study. In: Mohapatra D., Patnaik S. (eds) Intelligent Computing, Networking, and Informatics. Advances in Intelligent Systems and Computing, vol 243. Springer, New Delhi

53. Bineid, M. and Fielding, J.P. Development of a civil aircraft dispatch reliability prediction methodology, Aircraft Eng and Aerospace Tech, 2003, 75, (6), 2003, pp 588-594.

54. Nazeri, Z. and Jianping, Z. Mining aviation data to understand impacts of severe weather on airspace system performance, International Conference on Information Technology, 2002, IEEE.

55. Miaou SP. The relationship between truck accidents and geometric design of road sections–poisson versus negative binomial regressions, accident analysis and prevention, vol. 26. Elsevier; 1994.

56. Abdel-Aty MA, Radwan AE. Modeling traffic accident occurrence and involvement. Accid Anal Prev Elsevier. 2000;32.

57. Jones B, Janssen L, Mannering F. Analysis of the frequency and duration of freeway accidents in Seattle, accident analysis and prevention, vol. 23. Elsevier; 1991.

58. Miaou SP, Lum H. Modeling vehicle accidents and highway geometric design relationships, accident analysis and prevention, vol. 25. Elsevier; 1993

59. Yiyun Peng, Linda Ng Boyle. Commercial driver factors in run-of-road crashes [J]. Transportation Research Record, 2012: 128-132.

60. G. Wulf, P. A. Hancock, and M. Rahimi. Motorcycle Conspicuity: An Evaluation and Synthesis of Influential Factors [J]. Journal of Safety Research, 1989: 153-176.

61. Sunanda Dissanayake, Jian John Lu. Factors influential in making an injury severity difference to older drivers involved in fixed object-passenger car crashes [J]. Accident Analysis and Prevention, 2002: 609-618.

62. Ali S. Al-Ghamdi. Using logistic regression to estimate the influence of accident factors on accident severity [J]. Accident Analysis and Prevention, 2002: 729-741.

63. Sylvia S. Zajac, John N. Ivan. Factors influencing injury severity of motor vehicle-crossing pedestrian crashes in rural Connecticut [J]. Accident Analysis and Prevention, 2003: 369-379.
64. Fran H. Norris, B. Alex Matthews, Jasmin K. Riad. Characterological, situational, and behavioral risk factors for motor vehicle accidents: a prospective examination [J]. Accident Analysis and Prevention, 2000: 505-515.
65. Lord, Dominique, and Fred Mannering. "The statistical analysis of crash-frequency data: a review and assessment of methodological alternatives." Transportation Research Part A: Policy and Practice 44.5 (2010): 291-305.
66. Poch, Mark, and Fred Mannering. "Negative binomial analysis of intersection-accident frequencies." Journal of transportation engineering 122.2 (1996): 105-113.
67. Kumar S, Toshniwal D (2016). A data mining approach to characterize road accident locations. J Mod Transp, vol. 24(1), pp. 62–72.
68. T. Kohonen, Self-organized formation of topologically correct feature maps Biol. Cybern., 43 (1982), pp. 59–69
69. Agrawal R, Srikant R. Fast algorithms for mining association rules in large databases. In: Proceedings of the 20th International Conference on very large data bases; 1994. pp. 487–99.
70. Data source: https://data.gov.uk/dataset/road-traffic-accidents accessed on 24 October 2016.
71. https://www.faa.gov/data_research/accident_incident/
72. Akaike H. (1987) Factor analysis and AIC. Psychome, vol. 52:317–32.
73. Chaturvedi A, Green P, Carroll J. (2001) K-modes clustering. Journal of Classification, vol. 18, pp.35–55.
74. Depaire B, Wets G and Vanhoof K (2008) Traffic Accident Segmentation by means of Latent Class Clustering, Accident Analysis and Prevention, Elsevier, vol. 40.
75. Domingos P and Pazzani M (1997) On the optimality of the simple Bayesian classifier under zero-one loss". Machine Learning.,vol. 29: 103–137.
76. J. M. Pardillo-Mayora, C. A. Domínguez-Lira, R. Jurado-Piña, "Empirical calibration of a roadside hazardousness index for Spanish two-lane rural roads", Accident Analysis and Prevention, vol. 42, 2010, pp. 2018–2023.
77. Zhang, J., Lindsay, J., Clarke, K., Robbins, G., Mao, Y., 2000. Factors affecting the severity of motor vehicle traffic crashes involving elderly drivers in Ontario. Accident Anal. Prev. 32 (1), 117–125.

78. Lee C, Saccomanno F, Hellinga B (2002) Analysis of crash precursors on instrumented freeways. Transp Res Rec. doi:10. 3141/1784-01.

79. Chen W, Jovanis P (2000) Method for identifying factors contributing to driver-injury severity in traffic crashes. Transp Res Rec. doi:10.3141/1717-01

80. Shaw, M. J., Subramaniam, C., Tan, G. W., & Welge, M. E. (2001). Knowledge management and data mining for marketing. Decision Support Systems, 31(1), 127–137.

Publications related to thesis:

1. Tiwari, Prayag, Huy Dao, and Gia Nhu Nguyen. "Performance Evaluation of Lazy, Decision Tree Classifier and Multilayer Perceptron on Traffic Accident Analysis." Informatica 41.1 (2017).

2. Tiwari, Prayag, Sachin Kumar, and Denis Kalitin. "Road-User Specific Analysis of Traffic Accident Using Data Mining Techniques." International Conference on Computational Intelligence, Communications, and Business Analytics. Springer, Singapore, 2017.

3. Kumar, Sachin, Prayag Tiwari and Kalitin Vladimirovich Denis. "Augmenting Classifiers Performance through Clustering: A Comparative Study on Road Accident Data." IJIRR 8.1 (2018): 57-68. Web. 17 Nov. 2017. doi:10.4018/IJIRR.2018010104.

4. Tiwari P., Nguyen G.N., Prasad M., Pratama M., Ashour A.S., Dey N., Analysis of Airplane crash by utilizing Text Mining Techniques-Accepted in Acta Informatica.

5. K Sachin, Shemwal V.B., Solanki V., Tiwari P., K Denis. "A Conjoint Analysis of Road Accident Data using K-modes clustering and Bayesian Networks," Annals of Computer Science and Information System, Volume 10, 53-56.

6. Tiwari, P., Mishra, B. K., Kumar, S., & Kumar, V. (2017). Implementation of n-gram Methodology for Rotten Tomatoes Review Dataset Sentiment Analysis. International Journal of Knowledge Discovery in Bioinformatics (IJKDB), 7(1), 30-41. doi:10.4018/IJKDB.2017010103.

7. Tiwari P., Nguyen G.N., Kumar S., Yadav P., Ashour A.S., Dey N., Sentiment Analysis based on Russian and English Review Dataset-accepted in Statistical Analysis and Data Mining: The ASA Data Science Journal.

8. Prayag Tiwari. Article: Comparative Analysis of Big Data. International Journal of Computer Applications 140(7):24-29, April 2016. Published by Foundation of Computer Science (FCS), NY, USA.

9. P. Tiwari, "Improvement of ETL through integration of query cache and scripting method," 2016 International Conference on Data Science and Engineering (ICDSE), Cochin, India, 2016, pp. 1-5. doi:10.1109/ICDSE.2016.7823935.

10. P. Tiwari, "Advanced ETL (AETL) by integration of PERL and scripting method," 2016 International Conference on Inventive Computation Technologies (ICICT), Coimbatore, India,2016,pp.1-5.doi:10.1109/INVENTIVE.2016.7830102.

11. P. Tiwari, S. Kumar, A. C. Mishra, V. Kumar and B. Terfa, "Improved performance of data warehouse," 2017 International Conference on Inventive Communication and Computational Technologies (ICICCT), Coimbatore,India,2017,pp.94-104.doi:10.1109/ICICCT.2017.7975167.

Web of Science and Scopus indexed Publications

1. Tiwari, Prayag, Huy Dao, and Gia Nhu Nguyen. "Performance Evaluation of Lazy, Decision Tree Classifier and Multilayer Perceptron on Traffic Accident Analysis." Informatica 41.1 (2017).

2. Tiwari, Prayag, Sachin Kumar, and Denis Kalitin. "Road-User Specific Analysis of Traffic Accident Using Data Mining Techniques." International Conference on Computational Intelligence, Communications, and Business Analytics. Springer, Singapore, 2017.

3. Kumar, Sachin, Prayag Tiwari and Kalitin Vladimirovich Denis. "Augmenting Classifiers Performance through Clustering: A Comparative Study on Road Accident Data." IJIRR 8.1 (2018): 57-68. Web. 17 Nov. 2017. doi:10.4018/IJIRR.2018010104.

4. Tiwari P., Nguyen G.N., Prasad M., Pratama M., Ashour A.S., Dey N., Analysis of Airplane crash by utilizing Text Mining Techniques-Accepted in Acta Informatica.

5. K Sachin, Shemwal V.B., Solanki V., Tiwari P., K Denis. "A Conjoint Analysis of Road Accident Data using K-modes clustering and Bayesian Networks," Annals of Computer Science and Information System, Volume 10, 53-56.

6. Tiwari P., Nguyen G.N., Kumar S., Yadav P., Ashour A.S., Dey N., Sentiment Analysis based on Russian and English Review Dataset-accepted in Statistical Analysis and Data Mining: The ASA Data Science Journal.

7. P. Tiwari, "Improvement of ETL through integration of query cache and scripting method," 2016 International Conference on Data Science and Engineering (ICDSE), Cochin, India, 2016, pp. 1-5. doi:10.1109/ICDSE.2016.7823935.

8. P. Tiwari, S. Kumar, A. C. Mishra, V. Kumar and B. Terfa, "Improved performance of data warehouse," 2017 International Conference on Inventive Communication and Computational Technologies (ICICCT), Coimbatore,India,2017,pp.94-104.doi:10.1109/ICICCT.2017.7975167

9. V. Kumar, D. Kalitin, P. Tiwari, "Unsupervised Learning Dimensionality Reduction Algorithm PCA For Face Recognition," International Conference on Computing Communication and Automations (ICCCA)" proceeding will be published in IEEE-Xplore.

10. P. Tiwari, S. Kumar, A.C. Mishra, V. Kumar, B. Terfa, "Improved Performance of Data Warehouse," International Conference on Inventive Communication and Computational Technologies (ICICCT-2017), Coimbatore, 10-11 March 2017. Proceeding will be published IEEE-Xplore.